1 Contact and openness in permanent placement

Introduction

This guide examines practice experience and research findings regarding contact in permanent placements outside a child's family of origin. It highlights factors to be taken into account in exploring whether and how a child's welfare would be promoted by planning some form of contact within the placement and the implications for agency policy and practice.

Only a minority of children will remain looked after on a long-term basis (Millham *et al*, 1986). Most will return to live with their parents or other members of their birth families or move to independence. For these children and young people there is usually no question about the importance of maintaining links with their birth family and wider network although there may be practice issues about the frequency and location of meetings and who should be involved in contact (Cleaver, 1998). There is less certainty among practitioners and policy makers about the appropriateness and nature of contact for children who remain looked after or who are placed for adoption. The majority of the children concerned will be past infancy at the time of permanent placement. However, attention will also be given in this guide to contact in relation to the small number of children placed each year as infants (5% of all adoptions in 1996)*.

There is new legislation that promotes and supports continuity and staying connected for all adopted children. The 2002 Adoption and Children Act will come into force in 2004. The National Adoption Standards for England (2001) and the accompanying Regulations and Guidance emphasise the importance of consideration of contact with the birth family and other significant people as one of the steps towards adoption.

Defining openness and contact

The terms "openness" and "contact" are used by researchers and practitioners who have been exploring and developing alternatives to the closed or "exclusive" model of placement. However, they are sometimes used interchangeably and not on an agreed basis (for a discussion of terminology, see Triseliotis *et al*, 1997, Chapter 4).

Openness

In this guide, "*openness*" refers to practice developments which encompass a more *inclusive* approach. These may or may not involve direct or indirect contact between a child and/or her or his carers and members of the birth family. Aspects of openness other than contact include:

- involving birth family members in the choice of, or discussions about, the alternative family placement

- an exchange of information between birth family members and prospective carers prior to placement

- adopters and birth parents or other relatives meeting on a "one-off" basis, irrespective of whether there may be a plan for contact after the placement

- the noting of updating information, from one or more parties to an adoption placement, on agency files. It may have been agreed prior to the adoption to pass on significant information (for example, relating to a death or serious illness) when it is received or it may be held on file to be shared later if requested

- an acknowledgement that the child has two families.

These practices may facilitate planning for contact at a later stage. A Family Rights Group publication (Lindley, 1997) provides information about the extent to which policy and practice in 50 agencies involved birth parents in the adoption process, while Lowe *et al* (1999) describe the experiences of openness in 115 agencies in England and Wales. Without the spirit of openness, contact can be an anxious, stressful and unsatisfying experience for the child and both

---

*Ivaldi G, *Children Adopted from Care: An examination of agency adoptions in England – 1996*, BAAF, 1998

families. Openness, which is an attitude of mind, can enhance any kind of contact and compensate by offering continuity when contact is not possible. It is a way of "keeping the door open" and therefore keeping a child connected to her or his roots.

Contact

The term "*contact*" encompasses different forms of *direct or indirect communication* between a child and/or her or his carers and a range of people including birth parents, siblings, members of the extended family network and previous carers. As well as face-to-face contact, *direct contact* may involve the exchange of letters, cards, presents, audiotapes, videos and photographs or telephone calls. *Indirect contact* includes any communication which is exchanged via a third party, usually the adoption agency (often referred to as a "letterbox" arrangement). Indirect contact may be between the adults only and the child may or may not be aware that this is occurring.

As so many different forms of communication may be included under the umbrella term of contact, it is important to clarify exactly what is meant in relation to policy, and in discussion of specific arrangements in individual cases.

The Adoption Regulations, which come into force in October 2003, and the new forms to be issued in autumn 2003 by the Department of Health, make it obligatory to assess and define, in detail, the contact needs and arrangements for continuity for each child, when adoption is the plan.

The historical context

Prior to the 1970s in the UK, children who entered care as toddlers or older children were usually accommodated in foster care or residential homes. They were rarely placed for adoption, which was seen as appropriate only for infants.

Adoption and contact

It was exceptional for contact to be arranged between children adopted as infants and members of their birth families. There was an emphasis on secrecy. It was generally accepted that adoption necessitated complete severance of any form of contact in order to achieve 'a completely new start' (Houghton, 1972).

However, it should be noted that "kinship" and "tribal" adoption and inclusive forms of permanent placement remained common in societies where western influence on child care practices remained marginal (O'Collins, 1984).

As the number of infants being placed for adoption declined during the early 1970s, the "permanence movement" rapidly developed and at that time permanence was seen as synonymous with adoption (for further discussion of its origins and philosophy see Triseliotis *et al*, 1997, and for a discussion of current themes on permanence see BAAF Practice Note 33, *Planning for Permanence*, 1996). Contact emerged as a professional issue when many older children in the care system who were unable to return to live with birth relatives were regarded as eligible for placement for adoption. Older black children, who had hitherto been more often placed with foster carers than with adoptive parents, began to be placed for adoption in larger numbers, usually with white families: 'permanence for the black child now came to be synonymous with the concept of transracial adoption' (Weise, 1987).

As part of the adoption plan for all children there was usually an unquestioned assumption by workers and agencies of a termination of contact between children and birth relatives, as had been traditional in baby adoptions. Severance of links with birth relatives and the wider community had an added dimension for black children placed transracially (Mallows, 1991). There was an increase in the number of contested adoption applications (from 6% to 11% between 1979 and 1983). Criticism began to be voiced by the end of the 1970s about the legal framework which severely limited parents' rights to challenge a local authority's decisions over contact.

The Health and Social Services & Social Security Adjudication Act 1983 in England and Wales for the first time gave parents a right to challenge decisions to terminate access, as it was then called, and also provided a statutory code of practice on contact which required local authorities to allow access unless they could demonstrate it was not in the interests of the child's welfare. The Children Act 1989 in England and Wales finally gave recognition to the importance of promoting as well as maintaining contact and increased the rights of children, parents and other family members to seek contact.

Contents

Fostering and contact

Although local authorities have always had the power to enable families to have access to their children in foster care, the contact needs of children were rarely addressed in agency policy or practice. There was a rather passive approach where contact often, albeit unintentionally, simply withered away after weeks or months of a child's placement.

It was not until the late 1970s that research in foster care clearly demonstrated that contact is the "key to discharge" for children's return home (Fanshel and Shinn, 1978). The importance of active work within short-term placements to promote contact for return home was increasingly emphasised. Rowe and Lambert's (1976) landmark study, *Children who Wait*, was unequivocal about the importance of access as a facilitating factor for children who were reunited with their families. However, there continued to be less recognition of the role contact might play in improved long-term outcomes for children in foster care. For example, in supporting the development of the child's positive identity formation and the particular significance of this for transracially or transculturally placed black and minority ethnic children.

In some cases it is still assumed that an existing contact arrangement can continue without preparation, support or the management of issues concerning its appropriateness. There is strong evidence (Bilson and Barker, 1995) that without active planning and support for carers, children and birth families, contact in foster care can diminish significantly over time and indeed may be better maintained for children who are in residential placements.

Changing attitudes to openness

Recognition of the need for less secrecy in adoption has derived from practice experience:

- Lessons have been learned from counselling adopted adults who have found that the secrecy of the closed model has left them with unresolved questions about their family history, culture and identity. The importance of information about origins is now widely accepted in adoption practice (Triseliotis *et al*, 1997). Furthermore, with increasing knowledge about the implications of genetic inheritance, a means of communication will be increasingly important for medical information.

- Some birth parents who relinquished babies (such placements reached a peak in the 1960s), and other birth parents who have lost an older child to adoption more recently, have pressed for increasing openness, especially regarding information as to their child's well-being. Some hope for contact, particularly once their child reaches adulthood (Ward, 1991; Mullender, 1997, Howe *et al*, 1992).

- The complexity of the task of adoptive parents has been increasingly acknowledged, and some adopters have welcomed greater openness, for example, through a pre-adoption meeting with birth parents or other relatives (Stone, 1994).

- A child or young person's need for contact and openness is not static – arrangements should take account of each individual's changing needs and circumstances.

2 The purpose of contact in permanence

Contact arrangements should centre on the benefits for the *child*, whilst acknowledging the adults' wishes and feelings and meeting these as far as is consistent with promoting the child's welfare.

> *Contact may be of singular importance to the long-term welfare of the child: first, in giving the child the security of knowing that his parents love him and are interested in his welfare; secondly, by avoiding any damaging sense of loss to the child in seeing himself abandoned by his parents; thirdly, by enabling the child to commit himself to the substitute family with the seal of approval of the natural parents; and fourthly, by giving the child the necessary sense of family and personal identity. Contact, if maintained, is capable of reinforcing and increasing the chances of success of a permanent placement, whether on a long-term fostering basis or by adoption.*

(Judgment given by Simon Brown L J *Re E A Minor* (Care order: contact), 1993 quoted in DoH circular LAC (98) 20)

Functions of contact

Direct or indirect contact, with birth parents and/or other relatives or carers and significant others, may serve a number of different functions for the child, varying over time, by:

- enabling a child to develop a realistic understanding of the circumstances leading to separation (this may be particularly relevant in the case of parents who have learning difficulties or who experience mental distress)

- enabling a child to grieve his/her loss

- enabling a child to move on and develop an attachment to new carers with the blessing of her or his parents

- reassuring a child that the birth parents or other relatives continue to care about the child, which may enhance the child's self-esteem

- promoting stability in a new or existing placement by providing continuity and enabling connections to be maintained

- reassuring a child about the well-being of birth relatives, especially siblings whether they are living with birth relatives or in an alternative family (Wedge and Mantle, 1991)

- providing an opportunity for an adopted child or young person to gain more knowledge and understanding about her or his personal and family history and cultural background and giving a child a sense of socio-geneological connectedness (Owusu-Bempah *et al*, 1997).

- maintaining a flow of communication which could facilitate direct, perhaps face-to-face contact, in the future, if this is requested or agreed by the adopted or fostered person.

Additional factors

There may be additional factors to take into account in exploring the benefits of contact for children from minority ethnic groups, particularly those who have one black and one white parent (Prevatt Goldstein, 1997). A placement may reflect some but not all aspects of a child's heritage (ethnic origin, language, religion, dress and food) (Husain Sumpton, 1999). The research of Barn *et al* (1997) suggested that 'greater recognition of the complexity of ethnic diversity' was required. Additional input may be needed from community members, if not from birth relatives, to enable the child to develop a clearer understanding and knowledge about her or his origins. For children placed transracially, particularly those placed with carers who have no family or community links which reflect the child's ethnic and cultural background, contact with individuals outside the adoptive or foster family will be vital. Such contact can help to promote a child's positive sense of who she or he is and prevent the child growing up rejecting her or his ethnic and cultural origins.

Most intercountry adoptions are transracial and/or transcultural and adopters may need help to seek further information from, maintain contact or seek friendships with, people who are from the child's original community.* Many self-help groups for adopters try to maintain contact between adopted children and their culture or family background. However, intercountry adoption works best if the parents can develop an affinity with, and affection for, the donor country and community. This is even more important than trying to inculcate an interest in the child.

Birth fathers

Whenever possible, birth fathers should be involved at all stages of the placement process. They are much more likely to lose contact with children who are looked after than mothers, and sometimes less strenuous efforts appear to be made to maintain contact with them (Clapton, 1997). It seems that as a result of gender discrimination, the child's wishes concerning contact with birth fathers and other male family members are given less consideration, as are the father's own wish for contact. Lowe and Murch *et al* (1999) learned from a postal questionnaire completed by 226 adoptive families that 49% had some form of ongoing direct or indirect contact with birth mothers but only 22% with birth fathers. An increasing proportion of adult adoptees are now seeking contact with both birth parents (ONS, 1998).

Changing needs

Contact arrangements are likely to change over time in response to a child's changing needs: the frequency and location of face-to-face meetings may be varied, or the nature of contact may change, for example, from contact by letter to face-to-face meetings or vice versa.

Well managed contact arrangements are time consuming, especially when there are potential conflicts of interest. Corners cut risk further losses for the child. If resources allow, a separate worker for the birth family and an independent mediator, when needed, can have a beneficial effect on the quality of contact. The quality of communication between children and families will be more pertinent in every case than an emphasis on the number of contacts. If contact is rewarding for all concerned, how often? where? and when? can follow, can be varied and reviewed to meet the changing needs of the child. (For a detailed discussion of how often? where? and when? see Newman, 1995.)

*The Overseas Adoption Helpline is available for families and workers, telephone 0870 516 8742.

3 The legal framework

England and Wales

The Adoption Act 1976 contains no explicit provision for contact before or after adoption. The Children Act 1989, however, governs the duties of local authorities and voluntary organisations towards children they are looking after or accommodating and their families.

Local authority duties in relation to contact for looked after children

Local authorities have a duty under the Children Act 1989 (Schedule 2, Paragraph 15) to promote contact between a child being looked after and her or his parents, anyone else with parental responsibility, and relatives and friends, unless it is not reasonably practicable or consistent with the child's welfare to do so. The precise legal obligations in respect of contact will differ according to whether a child is accommodated by voluntary arrangement, in care, or subject to a freeing order (see below). All children who are placed by a local authority for adoption are "looked after" by that local authority until the adoption order is made, but duties imposed by the Arrangements for Placement of Children (General) Regulations 1991 apply to all looked after children *except* those placed for adoption. [The Adoption Agencies and Children (Arrangements for Placement and Reviews) (Miscellaneous Amendments) Regulations 1997.] Where children are not placed for adoption, the arrangements for contact come within the list of issues that must be part of the plan for the child, under the Arrangements for Placement Regulations. In all cases it is good practice to make clear plans for what contact is envisaged before the placement is made. Once children are placed for adoption, the local authority duties in relation to contact will still be governed by the appropriate provisions in the Children Act as outlined below.

a) Accommodated children

When a child is being accommodated at the parent's request, the local authority must allow the parents and anyone who has previously had parental responsibility "reasonable contact" with the child. The birth parents retain parental responsibility and the local authority has no power to over-ride their wishes. This situation is likely to pertain particularly in cases of babies being relinquished for adoption. A dispute over contact could, unless handled appropriately and sensitively, threaten the continuance of the placement and it is therefore essential to clarify everyone's hopes and expectations *before* placement.

b) Children in care under a court order

Section 34 of the Children Act requires the local authority to allow a child in care "reasonable contact" with his or her parents or guardian, anyone who previously had parental responsibility and anyone previously caring for the child under a High Court order. The same section also provides for the making of court orders regarding contact. Such an order may have been made at the same time as a care order, or it may be made later on the direct application to the court by the child, the local authority or the parents. Alternatively, the local authority or the child may apply for an order under section 34 (4), permitting the local authority to refuse all contact between the child and a person who would otherwise be entitled to "reasonable contact". Other individuals, for example, relatives or former carers, may seek the court's leave to make an application for a contact order under section 34 (3) of the Act.

Where there is an existing order for contact, and the local authority and the person entitled to contact under the order are able to reach agreement to vary the contact arrangement, the revised agreement should be set out in the form prescribed in the Contact with Children Regulations 1991. It should be noted that the child (if of sufficient understanding) must also agree.

c) Children subject to freeing orders

A freeing order supersedes a care order and any section 34 contact arrangements no longer apply. Children freed for adoption continue to be "looked after" by the local authority which has the freeing order and the local authority continues to have a duty under the Children Act to promote contact with 'any relative, friend, or other person connected with (the child)' unless this is not reasonably practicable or consistent with the child's welfare. Following a freeing order, the birth parents are regarded as "former" parents and lose their right to make section 8 applications for contact without leave of the court.

It is possible, although relatively uncommon, for the court to make a section 8 contact order at the same time as the freeing order. This may give rise to problems, as the local authority is not technically able to apply to *vary* a section 8 contact order although it may be possible to invoke the inherent jurisdiction of the court to deal with this difficulty. If an order for contact under section 8 has been made, it will automatically be ended by the making of an adoption order.

d) Placement for adoption of a looked after child

The provisions in Part III & Schedule 2 of the Children Act, including the contact provisions, continue to apply. For children in care, section 34 and any order made under it will continue to apply unless varied by agreement or court order.

e) Contact after adoption

Since adoption proceedings are "family proceedings" under the Children Act, a court hearing an adoption application may make a section 8 contact order, with the adoption order, in favour of the birth parents or other relatives, whether or not an application has been made for one. It is not known how common such contact orders are, but they are thought to be rare for two main (and connected) reasons:

- Case law has indicated that contact should not generally be imposed against the wishes of the adopters – in practice, a contact order which is resented by the adopters may not achieve the desired end (*Re C* (1988) 1 ALL ER 705).

- Under Section 1 (5) of the Children Act, the court should only make any order if it is satisfied that this is better for the child than making no order. If the adopters indicate that they are willing for contact to take place, it may be argued that it is inappropriate to make an order, since the desired contact will take place without it (*Re T* (1995) 2 FLR 251).

If no order is made at the time of the adoption hearing, the person seeking contact will only subsequently be able to apply for an order if the court gives leave. It has been suggested by the courts that where there is an agreement for contact, this should be noted in the court file. Should the adoptive parents subsequently refuse contact previously agreed, this will give the birth parent or other contact applicant grounds for arguing that at least leave to make an application should be granted (*Re T* (adopted children – contact) (1995) 2 FLR 597). Thomas *et al*, in a major research study (BAAF 1999), found that contracts mutually agreed by two families, and the child if appropriate, are more conducive to co-operative contact than court orders. But occasionally an order may be used creatively to protect a child. For example, a sister and brother who had been grossly abused by both parents felt reassured by an order limiting contact to indirect birthday and Christmas cards. They had feared that their parents would find them and abuse them wherever they were, and they had more faith in "the court" than in mere people.

f) Contact for children who are subject of residence orders

In the case of non-relatives, residence orders are most likely to have been made in favour of foster carers who have been caring for a looked after child for at least three years. A residence order determines with whom the child will live and confers parental responsibility on that person. The birth parents retain parental responsibility and contact arrangements would normally be negotiated between the birth parents or other relatives and the carer. A contact order under section 8 could be made alongside a residence order if this were better than making no order.

Duties of voluntary agencies with regard to contact

Where a child who is looked after by a local authority is placed through a voluntary agency, the same rules apply as for any other looked after child. But in cases where voluntary adoption agencies have made an adoption placement at the direct request of a child's parent(s) there are no legislative requirements regarding contact. Nevertheless, it is essential before making any placement to be clear about what, if any, contact is planned, and for any expectations to be understood by both the birth parents and the prospective adopters.

Scotland

In Scotland, there are various provisions regulating contact, whether between different parents and adults, or between the local authority and parents, etc., when the child is looked after away from home. The position and method of regulation depend on where the child is living, and who has responsibilities and rights for him/her. (References to Acts are: 1995 Act = Children (Scotland) Act 1995; 1978 Act = Adoption (Scotland) Act 1978.)

Looked after children placed away from home

If the child is looked after away from home, contact depends on the legal basis for keeping the child.

- If the child is looked after under section 25 of the 1995 Act, contact should be arranged between the local authority and the birth parent. If the birth parent is not happy with the contact arrangements, they can, of course, simply ask for the child to be returned to their care, but this may not be practical for many parents.

- If the child is subject to a supervision requirement (section 70 of the1995 Act), it is the Hearing which regulates contact and not the court. Any person, including the birth parent, who is not happy about informal contact arrangements needs to ask the Hearing to include a contact condition in the supervision requirement. Contact is one of the many things which panel members can put in a supervision requirement, as a condition.

- If the child is looked after by the local authority under a parental responsibilities order (PRO) (section 86 of the 1995 Act), there is a general legal expectation that the birth parent will have contact with the child (section 88). If there are problems with this, then the sheriff court will regulate the position. This could include refusal of contact if contact is not in the child's best interest.

For all looked after children, the local authority has a duty to promote contact with parents, *if* the contact is in the child's best interests (section 17(1)(c) of the 1995 Act).

Children freed or adopted

- If a child is freed for adoption (section 18 of the 1978 Act), then the birth parent has no parental responsibilities whatsoever. All rights and responsibilities have been terminated. This means that there is no right to contact, and the birth parent also has no right to return to court to ask for contact under section 11 of the 1995 Act.

- If the child has been adopted, the position of the birth parent is the same as in freeing. The birth parent normally has no rights under the 1978 Act, and has no right to go to court under section 11 of the 1995 Act, and no right to return to court to ask for it.

However, it is possible for a court to add a condition about contact when adoption is granted. *If* such a condition is added, the birth parent *can* go back to court in the future if there are problems about contact. However, if there is no such condition, the birth parent has no rights. The Court of Session has said (*B v C* 1996 SLT) that conditions in adoption will only be added 'in exceptional circumstances'. This means that, in normal situations where there may be some contact, whether direct or not, the adoption order would not normally have a formal condition about contact. The matter would go ahead informally and the birth parent would have no enforceable rights.

Therefore, once a child has been adopted, if there is no contact condition, the birth parent has no rights whatsoever to return to court to seek contact, under any provisions, either the Adoption (Scotland) Act 1978 or the Children (Scotland) Act 1995. The parent only has a limited right if there is a condition attached to the adoption order.

Other birth relatives of the child may, however, seek contact under section 11 of the 1995 Act. This means that a grandparent or sibling of an adopted child could seek contact, even though the birth parent cannot.

4 Research evidence

It is important to consider what evidence is available to guide practitioners, given recent developments towards greater openness and more frequent contact in permanent placements (Social Services Inspectorate, 1995). However, it should be noted that no large scale prospective studies have been completed, either in the UK or elsewhere, which offer comparison of outcomes for children placed with and without contact.

Some evidence from UK research on the possible benefits of greater openness and ongoing contact in permanent placements (excluding residence orders) is contained within studies of placement outcomes which were not concerned solely with the effects of contact. In addition to studies referred to above, the work of Fratter *et al* (1991, 1996), Lowe and Murch *et al* (1999), Neil (2002) and Macaskill (2002) is also relevant. Some of the cumulative evidence from research has been usefully collated and interpreted by Quinton *et al* (1997). They conclude that knowledge is limited due to the lack of systematic research focusing on the effects of contact on the outcomes of permanent placements:

> *The conclusion that can be drawn from the available research is that open adoption with contact can work amicably. Claims have been advanced on the benefits they bring to all parties but these claims have yet to be substantiated, beyond some evidence on the stability of placements.*

Quinton *et al* add:

> *There is no evidence to support the idea that there are some future benefits to be gained by pushing for contact, when this seems against sense or experience... In our present state of knowledge it is seriously misleading to state that what we know about contact is at a level of sophistication to allow us to make confident assertions about the benefits to be gained from it, regardless of family circumstances and relationships.*

Two years later, Lowe and Murch *et al* (1999) come to the conclusion that research about contact does not have definitive messages:

> *... we should make it absolutely clear that we are by no means committed to the view that any form of contact between the child and the birth family is always in the child's interest. On the contrary, we take the view that the issue of contact must be governed by the welfare of the particular child (including taking into account the child's own wishes and feelings) in his or her circumstances, which may change from time to time. What has to be avoided is the imposition of inflexible rules based on doctrinaire policies.*

It seems that what we can learn from research is that good contact arrangements must fulfil a purpose which, in turn, must be rooted in a childcare plan based on careful assessment of each case, sensitive preparation, and enough support.

5 Key factors to be taken into account when considering contact

In exploring whether contact would be likely to promote the well-being of a child to be placed permanently outside the family of origin, workers will be drawing on the information which has been compiled for the Adoption and Permanent Placement Panel about the child's family and personal history, ethnic and cultural background, educational and medical needs, and overall development. They will also need to recognise the impact of their personal values and attitudes towards contact in making assessments. Equally it would be relevant to consider all of these factors in relation to a child living in what is currently an "exclusive" (closed) placement in which the possibility of initiating or resuming contact is being explored, and when the benefits of existing contact are being reviewed. The assessment should include the following:

- The child's wishes and feelings regarding contact; relationships with birth family members including siblings; emotional and developmental functioning; psychological resilience and ability to form or extend attachments.

- The relationship of the birth relatives with their child; their views about the plan for family placement and about contact; their previous experience of contact; their health and emotional well-being and their current functioning.

- The views and experience of the current carers in relation to contact.

- A clear sense of the purpose of any proposed contact for the child, in particular, whose needs would it be meeting?

- The attitudes and understanding of the potential carer(s) regarding contact and how they could meet the child's assessed needs for any direct or indirect contact.

- Any conflict inherent in the proposed plan and how this is to be addressed.

- What administrative, practical, financial, emotional or other support (including mediation or supervision) may be needed, at least initially, to facilitate any planned contact.

- What arrangement is in place for reviewing the agreement and negotiating over time so that

appropriate changes to the plan can be proposed and agreed by all parties, based on the child's changing needs and wishes and the circumstances of both families.

The child

A child's own wishes and feelings must be ascertained and taken into account, having regard to her or his age and degree of understanding. This work should be appropriate to the child's, emotional strength and development and sensitive to particular issues which may arise in relation to the child's ethnic and cultural background and any impairments or other special needs. McCauley's work (1996) indicates that children's views are not always regarded.

The assessment of the relationship between a child and her or his parents and other relatives will be critical in making future contact plans, as required by the new regulations. Sometimes the potential role of a birth father without parental responsibility and his relatives is overlooked. In assessing relationships, account must be taken of a child's disabilities or learning difficulties (Russell, 1995). An assessment will also need to be made of a child's relationships with siblings (whether adopted or fostered separately or living with birth relatives) and wider family network. For black children, the relationship with members of the extended family or community may be particularly important because family life may be less centred on the nuclear family:

> *Multiple mothering is a healthy and accepted pattern of family organisation among black people.* (Pennie and Best, 1990).

Relatives who have not had a close relationship with the child (this may be likely in the case of very young children or infants) may nonetheless be able to offer information, support and affection during childhood or later.

> *With very young children it may seem to adopters that contact meetings are of little point or value to the child as he or she is not asking*

questions about adoption. What is likely to help such adopters persist with contact is an understanding that the child will need to address questions of identity in the future. In my research, adopters who showed a good understanding of the lifelong needs of their child were more highly motivated to sustain contact as they had long term goals in mind. (Neil, E 2002)

For some children, maintaining their relationship with previous foster carers may be important. However, where there has been disagreement or conflict between foster and adoptive carers, or where foster carers may have hoped to care for the child on a permanent basis, they may not feel able to offer support to the new placement. It is vital that the adults are given the support and opportunity to air their feelings honestly and that an assessment is made as to whether any unresolved feelings are likely to jeopardise the new placement, should contact continue. It is important that a child has the carer's permission to move on, but it is equally important that all the adults tell the same story.

Understanding the child's attachment history is an essential part of assessing contact needs. Yet Eurocentric perceptions of attachment theory can exclude the value and diversity of different cultural patterns. It is necessary to maintain clarity regarding the emotional and developmental needs of children along with an awareness about different ways in which these can be met.

It is the quality of a child's attachments to significant adults that can best inform plans for contact. A child who has experienced good pre-permanent placement care will generally make a more secure attachment to new carers in time, and be able to sustain multiple attachments. Children who have experienced poor care from depressed, ambivalent or abusing adults will often bring with them dysfunctional and disorganised patterns of attachment which require careful observation and interpretation. Whether children with early damaged attachments are helped by continuing contact with birth parents or previous carers will depend very much on the nature of that relationship and whether it helps to reinforce the new attachment rather than undermine the new carers. In some circumstances ongoing contact may inhibit healing, recovery and the development of alternative, healthier ways of relating especially following severe trauma and/or abuse.

There can be no substitute for a careful assessment of the child's individual history, attachments and network of relationships. Children may well have attachments of different quality even with their primary attachment figures and the significance of secondary attachments (e.g. siblings, close extended family, friends) should not be underestimated. Workers may find it useful to refer to Fahlberg's (1994) observations on attachment when undertaking their assessment. The following vignette encapsulates some of the dilemmas that social workers have to balance.

Jason

Jason is seven. He has been in care since he was two and has spent four of the past five years with his foster carers who have now stated that they wish to adopt him. His mum died a year ago. Despite chronic alcohol and drug misuse, she did maintain good quality contact with him. His dad is addicted to heroin but maintains contact with Jason somewhat inconsistently about once every month.

Jason is presently having weekly play therapy to help him grieve for the double loss of his mother. He has made it clear by both his words and his behaviour that he wants to remain with his carers but he also wants to retain close links with his dad and with the extended family of both his parents.

The carers can only see contact in negative terms – the criminal culture of the extended family, and Jason's anguish and response to his dad's inconsistent visits. They have stated that they do not want contact to continue in any form.

Jason's worker feels that she is being asked to make an impossible decision between the long term security of this placement and Jason's right and desire for contact.

She discusses the problem with the foster carers and Jason's father in terms of Jason's need for both continuity and stability: continuity which is represented by contact with his family of origin and stability which can only be provided by the foster carers. The play therapist also sees the father and the foster carers to explain how Jason is expressing these needs. She stresses how valuable it would be for his further development if the adults he cares about could work together.

Following these discussions, there is a group conference with the foster carers, Jason's father, his social worker, the family link worker and an independent mediator. The foster carers are able to tell the father how angry they were every time Jason was let down or upset by unreliable visits and they admit that they feel threatened by Jason's conflict of loyalties. The father is able to say how intimidated he feels by the foster carers but also how grateful he is to them for looking after Jason so well. He assures them that he will support the adoption but he wants to go on seeing Jason. Both social workers confess that the problems about contact were predictable and that they have not given enough time to prepare and support everyone concerned.

It is agreed that future visits will focus on an activity which the father will be invited to join: picnics, shopping expeditions, birthday teas, football matches and other family outings are suggested by the foster carers. The social workers agree to liaise, to monitor and to review on a three monthly basis.

Contact continues and adoption plans proceed. There are some difficulties and some disappointments for Jason, but the foster carers feel that, on balance, Jason and the placement are gaining from the new arrangements which are less prescriptive and more enjoyable than the old monthly visits. They no longer regard contact as an imposition but more as keeping in touch with a family friend who can, on occasions, be tiresome. Jason's father is more confident because he is more sure of a welcome and Jason feels less inhibited now about wanting to see his father and also wanting to be adopted.

Parents and birth relatives

Permanent placements outside the family of origin may be provided because birth parents and relatives cannot meet a child's special needs; or because they have been unable, despite support, to offer adequate care; or because of a combination of these factors.

Although parents of, for example, a child with disabilities may feel unable to provide full-time care, they may wish to remain as concerned adults in their child's life. There could be mutual benefits from continuing contact in such circumstances (Fratter, 1996, Macaskill 2002).

More commonly, parents' own ill-health or mental distress, or neglectful or abusive behaviour, may have led to their children being placed with permanent families from the care system. This does not in itself mean every form of contact would be unacceptable, but there may be circumstances which can make future contact potentially damaging to the child.

Some children come from backgrounds where there is a network of abuse which has distorted the family relationships to such an extent that the child could potentially be in danger of further abuse as a result of contact. Children who have been subjected to sexual abuse within dysfunctional families may suffer from severe emotional trauma if contact is encouraged, or even if the whereabouts of their new carers is known (Smith, 1995). It can be extremely difficult to monitor and supervise even indirect contact in the form of letters, as these can include coded messages only understood by the recipients. However, some form of communication may be possible in these circumstances with a relative who has not been part of an abusive relationship.

Bonding – or the capacity of the parent to nurture – is a further important consideration in planning contact. Premature and stereotyped assumptions regarding parents with disabilities, learning difficulties, addictions, etc, are unhelpful. Again, the quality of the attachment is the key factor and when contact is seen to be in a child's best interests it requires proactive support for all concerned. However, research (Gibbons et al, 1995) does indicate that parenting which is characterised by low warmth/high criticism is particularly damaging to children's well being. There may be situations when the adult's capacity to interact with the child is so limited or unhealthy that contact cannot be positively sustained.

In exploring the possibility of some form of contact with a birth relative, it will be important to take account of diverse family structures, particularly among black and minority ethnic families.

Each family has its own system, writes its own script and creates its own myths (Lindsey, 1995). When children are placed with unrelated permanent carers two systems meet, and if there is to be contact, they must learn to understand and accommodate each other. It is part of the preparation for placement to evaluate how any two systems might affect a desired contact plan. For instance, what does each family mean by "keeping in touch"? Differences in ethnic and cultural background, class, educational achievement, socio-economic circumstances and child care practices may all aggravate tensions associated with contact.

Some birth parents have a disability and require special support to maintain contact, others may simply not be able to keep to a plan, however much they were consulted beforehand. It takes strength and confidence to sustain a relationship with a child living in another family. If all the birth parents with children in care were strong and confident, their children would not need to be placed with alternative carers in the first place. Parents who have the best intentions may therefore need an unforeseen amount of help to continue to make a contribution to their child's life.

Much of the research about contact emphasises the importance of birth relatives' attitude to their child's placement. Lindley (1998) identifies

> ...the need for evidence that the visiting parent will not be resentful of the adoptive parents and will not disrupt the placement, or where they are showing ambivalence about it, that the visiting relative has potential to work with and overcome residual feelings of resentment.

While adoptive parents can feel confirmed in their role if birth parents give their blessing, they may feel undermined by hostility or criticism.

Parents or other relatives of looked after children who, because of their own personal difficulties or lifestyle, are inconsistent and unable to fulfil contact arrangements are likely to risk causing distress to their child. It is vital to establish the reasons why contact is not being maintained and to ensure that there are not any practical or emotional reasons which are obstacles to contact, such as distance, transport difficulties, travel or other costs; feelings of guilt or loss; or ambivalence towards contact by the child's carers (Cleaver, 1998).

Kinship placements

> Of the advantages that kinship care offers, promoting good quality long-term links with a child's mother and father must be one of the greatest; but it is here too that the complexity can be greatest. (Pitcher, D 2002)

Children are usually placed with grandparents, aunts, uncles or other relatives at a time of family crisis and confusion. Good quality contact will not happen just because it's "in the family". All the usual assessments will have to be made with special reference to family conflicts and alliances and to the inevitable changes in established relationships, which follow a kinship placement. It is, of course, vital that families are enabled to make their own informed decisions and arrangements for contact with readily available social work support. There is a misguided belief – especially regarding black kinship placements – that family ties and connections will be automatically preserved.

> Yet serious role conflicts can arise for all kinship carers who have to cope with their own emotions, demands from the child, parents and extended family (Galloway, H and Wallace, F 2002)

The views and experiences of the current carers in relation to contact

Bridge or short-term carers may have observed contact between a child and birth relatives and her or his reactions to this. Their perceptions may be helpful in informing the assessment but due regard should be given to individual circumstances which may affect their view: their own family system, past experiences of contact, attitudes/feelings towards a particular child and parents and weight they may give to certain factors such as the importance of sibling relationships.

Whose needs would be met by contact?

Decisions for contact should be made in the best interests of the child and the benefits to all parties, direct and indirect, clearly identified. It should be noted that the child may benefit, sometimes indirectly, if contact is helpful to adoptive parents or to birth parents. For example, adopters may feel more confident about their role if they have positive contact with a birth relative, while a birth parent who feels reassured about her or his child's well-being, may be more supportive of the placement. However, contact should not be used as a bargaining tool, nor as a substitute to working with issues of loss.

The attitudes and understanding of permanent carers regarding contact

All prospective carers being recruited for permanent fostering and adoption should be invited to discuss how the continuity needs of the children they hope to have can be met in the present and in the future. Contact plans should be a crucial factor in Panel consideration of a link between a child and prospective carers. Permanent carers should be committed to fulfilling the assessed needs of the child for direct or indirect contact and be open to the possibility of changes in contact patterns in the years ahead. Whether or not contact is planned in the foreseeable future, openness of attitude on the part of adoptive parents or foster carers is likely to be valued by the child and contribute to a positive experience of contact if it happens. As long as there is openness, carers should not feel they have failed the child if contact cannot be established.

While agencies have become more ready to plan for some kind of contact in permanent placements, difficulties have arisen about carers' willingness to fulfil contact arrangements, once the child is in placement, despite information about the benefits of contact during preparation (Lowe and Murch *et al*, 1999). This points to the value of involving permanent carers in the initial decisions about meeting contact needs. It is both easier and more imperative for people to carry out plans if they feel partly responsible for them. It also happens that carers can become more enthusiastic about contact than social workers if they are really encouraged to act on behalf of the child.

Black adoptive and foster carers may well be more receptive to contact but this should not be taken for granted. The study by Thoburn *et al* (2000) suggests that whereas during the 1980s white carers were more likely to associate adoption with a severance of contact with birth relatives, it was 'more common for African-Caribbean or Asian parents to tell us that they did not consider it appropriate to cut off

contact'. White adoptive or foster carers with children from other ethnic groups, including intercountry adopters, will increasingly have to acknowledge the child's connection to a birth family and a community.

Arrangements for review

At some stage there may be a request by the child, the birth parent or the carer for a change to the contact arrangements. For looked after children there is a review system whereby arrangements can be changed following consultation with all parties. For children who have been adopted, the new legislation places a duty on agencies to review the purpose of, and the arrangements for, contact as part of its obligatory adoption support services.

Difficulties caused by a lack of contact which the child wants or needs are often overlooked. Children may feel it is their own fault when one or other party refuses contact. Some birth relatives may be unable or unwilling to maintain contact. Despite prior agreement, adopters may refuse to allow contact between the new child and her or his siblings adopted elsewhere or living with birth relatives. The latter may be a particularly difficult situation for the child, who is frequently singled out as the only child rejected, and isolated not only from their birth parents but also their siblings. These children have been identified in studies as having particular difficulties in coming to terms with the rejection and attaching to a new family (Quinton *et al*, 1997). All of these factors would require consideration in reviewing contact arrangements. It may, therefore, be helpful to include a mechanism for extra reviews on request in any contact agreement.

The following vignettes describe situations that social workers will be familiar with. It may help the reader to take a new look at these stories as they try to apply theory to their complicated real life practice.

The Smith family

There are six children in the Smith family ranging in age from three to 14. A year ago their father was convicted of physically and sexually abusing his oldest son (14) and daughter (12). During the investigation it became clear that there was a culture of sibling abuse and distorted relationships within this fairly isolated family.

All six children are now being looked after in a combination of residential and foster care arrangements. Their mother, who acknowledges that she is not able to protect her children from abuse, wants to meet with all of them together at least once a week. The children's view seems to concur with this although the behaviour of the youngest two who are aged three and five would suggest that they are ambivalent. After a year of supervised contact it is clear that these children are unlikely to live together as a family again.

In relation to the child care plans, what is the purpose of contact, for each sibling, with the mother?

What is the purpose of contact for each sibling with other siblings?

How much does the children's need for continuity and remaining connected to their birth family depend on direct contact?

Will direct contact reinforce or hinder their availability to work on loss and abuse?

Do any of the siblings need respite from direct contact to give time for healing?

Do the siblings support each other as a group or do they undermine each other?

Can all the children retain relationships in their minds? For how long?

How do the family systems, in which the children are placed, influence contact arrangements?

Will attempts at re-education to form healthy attachments be strengthened or weakened by contact?

How can the future arrangements for contact fulfil the stated purpose of contact for each child?

Laurie

Laurie is seven and has been with his current "short-term" foster carers since he was four. They are in their late 50s and are willing to look after him for as long as he wants to or they are able to.

Laurie's birth family has lost contact and cannot be found. He has no recollection of his parents. Laurie is almost entirely unattached to anyone or to anything. Apart from this, his behaviour is not difficult. His current carers are saddened but not perturbed by his detachment and see their role as providing him with 'a safe boundary within which he can roam about'.

Following referral to Be My Parent, the local authority have identified a suitable adoptive family for Laurie, a long distance away from where he has lived for the first seven years of his life. The current carers are willing to respond to any overtures for contact that Laurie will initiate in the future but would not want to initiate any contact themselves.

Have the prospective adopters been encouraged to consider all of Laurie's needs, which would surely include his need for contact with his foster carers?

Will the foster carers be involved with preparing the adopters so that Laurie can observe that the adults co-operate to take care of him?

Do both sets of parents understand that Laurie may not be able to express or even to comprehend his own needs and that the adults hold responsibility to preserve continuity for a child?

Will financial help, if required, be available for the foster carers to visit Laurie in his new home and for the adopters to take Laurie to his old home?

Will the adopters be able to keep the door open for Laurie's birth family and to offer him continuity by including them in his life despite their absence?

6 Implications for agencies

The adoption legislation in England and Wales as well as in Scotland increasingly recognises the importance of adoption support for all parties to adoption. Demands for post-adoption support have increased and the growing number of direct and indirect contact arrangements are a contributory factor. Lowe and Murch *et al* (1999) found that 95% of agencies had a system for the exchange of information between the adoptive families and the child's birth family. Agency policies, procedures and practice guidelines need to reflect both the intention of the new legislation and the growing openness in adoption practice.

Some key points relating to policy and procedures are summarised below:

- Consideration needs to be given to the potential benefits of openness for each child, including the possibility of direct or indirect contact, when plans for permanent placement and Panel reports are being produced. The new DoH forms, to be issued later in 2003, have extensive sections on contact which must be completed as part of the adoption plan. A child's need for contact should be an important factor in identifying suitable carers. In relation to the placement of infants, adopters and birth parents may meet prior to adoption, and arrangements for indirect contact may be set up, but it is unusual for face-to-face contact to continue after placement. Guidelines will need to be developed regarding criteria for decisions about promoting a child's welfare through post-placement and post-adoption contact, particularly in relation to infant adoptions.

- The involvement of birth family members in the planning process should include discussion of whether some form of contact with one or more family members would contribute to the child's well-being, in the short term or in the future. Support to birth relatives during the process of adoption, particularly when there has been opposition to the plan, should include helping them to understand their changed role in relation to the child. The use of an external worker/agency may be necessary for this work.

- Recruitment, preparation and training of permanent carers will need to take account of more open practice, so that carers are prepared to encourage and support continuing contact whenever appropriate for the child.

- Especially in inter-agency placements, a written contact agreement, negotiated with all the parties, should set out the nature and form of any contact, together with the role, if any, of each agency; the system for monitoring and reviewing the agreement; and the arrangements for dealing with any dissatisfaction or departures from the agreement (see Lindley, 1998, for a model post-adoption contact agreement). An SSI report (1996) described how the absence of such an agreement was found to cause confusion and anger for birth families because the extent of contact had not been specified clearly or monitored sufficiently. Although not legally binding, an agreement does provide a record which can be referred back to in the event of any changes or disagreements in the future.

- A system should be in place for the exchange of information via the agency, including arrangements for providing guidance to adoptive parents and birth relatives about the content of letters and monitoring (see Lindley, 1998, for a letterbox service flow chart).

- Adoption support services should provide, if needed, mediation where difficulties have arisen or to assist in re-negotiating a contact arrangement; support for the child, the carers or adoptive parents or birth relatives in relation to contact; and financial or practical resources. There are difficulties inherent in monitoring; in reality it may be the adopters or foster carers who are left with the responsibility of ensuring that contact, whether direct or indirect, is maintained. As part of an adoption support service, practitioners may facilitate the setting up of support groups, provide information about self-help organisations or make a referral to specialist services.

- A system for hearing the child's views should be enshrined in policy. Children know who the significant people are in their lives and whom they need to see to stay connected. It could be a distant aunt, a teacher, a friend or a foster carer from the past as well as parents, grandparents, sisters and brothers.

- Practitioners should be assisted through agency guidelines to respond to enquiries from any member of the adoptive family, including the child, or from a birth relative, seeking information. Sometimes there may be a need to pass on specific information which it is important for either the child or the birth parent/relative to know.

7 Conclusions

The development of greater openness in adoption and permanent foster care in the UK has occurred within a context of social change, particularly in relation to broader understanding of what constitutes a "family". Dimmock (1998), writing about the contemporary stepfamily, refers to the diversity and range of family forms:

African and African-Caribbean families ... seem less concerned about 'birth ownership'.

He argues that:

Successful and inclusive families (of whatever type) are a vital model because they challenge society to accept that all adults have a measure of parental responsibility for all children.

While some form of contact can be incorporated into a permanent placement for the benefit of the child and to the satisfaction of the adults concerned, it is important to note that direct contact may not be appropriate for all children, nor at all stages in their development. While some may wish to maintain contact with their birth families, there will also be a proportion for whom direct contact will not be appropriate, because of the nature of the breakdown of their relationship with their birth family. Even if there is no direct or indirect contact, there can still be continuity for the child, stemming from an open attitude within the foster or adoptive family. A child should never be expected to sever his or her connections to his/her family of origin – there is no such thing as "a fresh start". There is limited experience of the impact of direct contact in baby adoptions, and the outcome of longitudinal and large scale research is still awaited.

Agency guidelines must allow for the individual circumstances of each case. The fundamental principle that must underlie negotiation and decision-making is that contact should focus on the best interests of the child, enhancing a child's well-being, particularly in the areas of self-esteem and identity. The provision of contact is no substitute for work with a child and/or birth parent on issues of loss and change. Arrangements for contact (or for no contact) are likely to need to be reviewed and changed as the child grows older and/or circumstances change.

Careful assessment of the child's wishes and feelings will be a helpful starting point in most negotiations around contact, with recognition of any special issues arising from, for example, a child's experience of racism. In the case of some very young children or children with learning difficulties, practitioners have a particular responsibility to weigh all the factors carefully in making an assessment.

Factors which have to be taken into account for a satisfactory experience of contact for the various parties include the relationship of parents or other relatives with the child and the child's attachments to them; the attitude of birth relatives to the placement and the role they anticipate playing in the child's life; the feelings and understanding of the prospective carers about contact; and the possibility of a mutually respectful relationship between the adults involved in the child's life. Differences in class, ethnic origin, culture and gender are likely to be relevant. For example, it is sometimes the adoptive parent of the same gender as a birth parent with contact who feels uneasy or threatened by contact, rather than her or his partner.

For agencies the monitoring, reviewing and administration of contact arrangements form an ever increasing part of their adoption support services. In all cases there will be a right for ongoing access to social work, financial or practical support or mediation. However, understanding the lifetime needs of the child by all the adults concerned in planning, participating in, or supporting contact will be the key factor in determining successful outcomes.

The experiences reported by those directly involved in permanent placements, including adopted children and young people, indicate that various forms of direct or indirect contact can contribute positively to some, but by no means all, such placements. It is to be hoped that both longitudinal research and longer term practice experience will indicate more clearly the circumstances in which contact is likely to be beneficial.

8 References

Argent H (ed) (1995) *See You Soon: Contact with children looked after by local authorities*, London: BAAF.

BAAF Practice Note 33, *Planning for Permanence.*

Barn R, Sinclair R and Ferdinand D (1997) *Acting on Principle: An examination of race and ethnicity in social services provision for children and families*, London: BAAF.

Bilson A and Barker R (1993) 'Parental contact with children fostered and in residential care after the Children Act 1989', *British Journal of Social Work*, 25

Booth T and Booth W (1994) *Exceptional Childhoods, Unexceptional Children: Growing up with parents who have learning difficulties*, Family Policy Studies Centre in association with the Joseph Rowntree Trust.

Clapton G (1997) 'Birth fathers, the adoption process and fatherhood', in *Adoption & Fostering* 21:1.

Cleaver H (1997/1998) 'Contact: the social worker's experience', in *Adoption & Fostering* 21:4.

Dimmock B (1997/98) 'The contemporary stepfamily: making links with fostering and adoption', in *Adoption & Fostering* 21:4, pp 49-55.

Dutt R and Sanyal A (1991) 'Openness in adoption or open adoption – a Black perspective', in *Adoption & Fostering* 15:4, pp 111-115.

Fahlberg V (1994) *A Child's Journey Through Placement*, London: BAAF.

Fanshel D and Shinn E B (1978) *Children in Foster Care*, NY: Columbia University Press, USA.

Fratter J (1996) *Adoption with Contact: Implications for policy and practice*, London: BAAF.

Fratter J, Rowe J, Sapsford D and Thoburn J (1991) *Permanent Family Placement*, London: BAAF.

Galloway H and Wallace F (2002) 'Managing contact arrangements in black kinship care' in Argent H (ed) *Staying Connected*, London: BAAF

Houghton (Chair) (1972) *Report of the Departmental Committee on the Adoption of Children*, Home Office and Scottish Education Department, Cmnd 5107, para 29.

House of Commons (1984) *Children Act 1975: Second Report to Parliament*, DHSS/Welsh Office: HMSO.

Howe D (1995) *Attachment Theory for Social Work Practice*, Macmillan.

Howe D, Sawbridge P and Hinings D (1992, 1997) *Half a Million Women*, Penguin, Post Adoption Centre.

Husain Sumpton A (1999) 'Communicating with and assessing black children', in Barn R (ed), *Working with Black Children and Adolescents in Need*, BAAF.

Lindley B (1997) *Secrets or Links? Report on a Trawl of Adoption Agency Practice*, Family Rights Group.

Lindley B (1998) *Partnership with Birth Families in the Adoption Process*, Family Rights Group.

Lindsey C (1995) 'Systemic and developmental aspects of contact', in Argent H (ed), *See You Soon*, London: BAAF.

Lowe N, Murch M, Borkowski M, Weaver A, Beckford V and Thomas C (1999) *Supporting Adoption: Reframing the approach*, London: BAAF.

Macaskill C (2002) *Safe Contact? Children in Permanent Placement and Contact with their Birth Relatives*, Lyme Regis: Russell House Publishing

Macaskill C (2002) 'Managing contact arrangements for children with learning difficulties' in Argent H (ed) *Staying Connected*, London: BAAF

Mallows M (1991) 'Transracial adoption – the most open adoption', in Mullender A (ed), *Open Adoption: The philosophy and the practice*, London: BAAF.

Marriage and Divorce Statistics, ONS, Series SM2, No 22.

McCauley C (1996) *Children in Long Term Foster Care: Emotional and Social Development*, Avebury.

Millham S, Bullock R, Hosie K and Haak M (1986) *Lost in Care: The problems of maintaining links between children in care and their families*, Dartington Social Research Unit.

Mullender A and Kearn S (1997) *"I'm Here Waiting": Birth relatives' views on part 11 of the Adoption Contact Register for England and Wales*, London: BAAF.

Neil E (2002) 'Managing face-to-face contact for young adopted children' in Argent H (ed) *Staying Connected*, London: BAAF

Newman R (1995) 'From access to contact in a local authority setting' in Argent H (ed), *See You Soon*, London: BAAF.

O'Collins M (1984) 'The influence of western adoption laws on customary adoption in the third world', in Bean P (ed), *Adoption: Essays in social policy, law and sociology*, Tavistock.

Owusu-Bempah J and Howitt D (1997) 'Socio-genealogical connectedness, attachment theory, and childcare practice', *Child and Family Social Work* vol. 2, pp 199-207.

Pennie P and Best F (1990) *How the Black Family is Pathologised by the Social Services Systems*, Association of Black Social Workers and Allied Professionals.

Pitcher D (2002) 'Is Mummy coming to-day?' in Argent H (ed) *Staying Connected*, London: BAAF.

Prevatt Goldstein B (1997) 'Black children with one white parent: A parent's perspective' in *Selected Seminar Papers 1995/96*, London: BAAF.

Quinton D, Rushton A, Dance C and Mayes D (forthcoming) *Joining New Families: Establishing permanent placements in middle childhood*, Wiley and Sons.

Quinton D, Rushton A, Dance C and Mayes D 'Contact between children placed away from home and their birth parents: research issues and evidence', *Clinical Child Psychology and Psychiatry*, 2:3, pp 393-413.

Rowe J and Lambert L (1973) *Children Who Wait*, London: Association of British Adoption Agencies.

Russell P (1995) 'The importance of contact for children with disabilities – Issues for Policy and Practice' in Argent H (ed), *See You Soon*, London: BAAF.

Ryburn M (ed) (1994) *Contested Adoptions: Research, law, policy and practice*, Arena.

Ryburn M (ed) (1994) *Open Adoption: Research, theory and practice*, Avebury.

Smith G (1995) 'Do children have a right to leave their pasts behind them?', in Argent H (ed), *See You Soon*, London: BAAF.

Social Services Inspectorate, Department of Health (1995) *Moving Goalposts: A study of post adoption contact in the north of England*, HMSO.

Social Services Inspectorate (1996) *For Children's Sake: An SSI inspection of local authority adoption services*, HMSO.

Stone S (1994) 'Contact between adopters and birth parents: The Strathclyde experience', *Adoption & Fostering* 18:2, pp 36-38.

Thoburn J, Murdoch A and O'Brien A (1986) *Permanence in Child Care*, Blackwell.

Thoburn J, Norford L and Rashid S (2000) *Permanent Family Placement for Children of Minority Ethnic Origin*, University of East Anglia/DoH.

Thomas C and Beckford V with Murch M and Lowe N (1999) *Adopted Children Speaking*, London: BAAF.

Triseliotis J, Shireman J and Hundleby M (1997) *Adoption: Theory, policy and practice*, Cassell.

Ward D (1991) 'Closed adoption – a lifetime loss', in Mullender A (ed), *Open Adoption: The philosophy and the practice,* London: BAAF.

Wedge P and Mantle G (1991) *Sibling Groups and Social Work*, University of East Anglia.

Weise J (1987) *Trans-racial Adoption: A Black Perspective*, University of East Anglia: Monograph Series.

Books on Contact from BAAF

Staying Connected: Managing contact in adoption
Edited by Hedi Argent

Making and managing contact arrangements with birth parents, wider birth family members and other people who are significant to the child is a hugely complex and challenging task. All the contributors to this anthology are involved in making, sustaining or evaluating contact arrangements and they offer examples of varied practice to explore what works and what does not and why.

BAAF 2002   244PP   ISBN 1 903699 12 6   £12.95 + £3.50 P&P

Safe Contact?
Children in permanent placement and contact with their birth relatives
Catherine Macaskill

This book considers the impact of face-to-face contact on adopted children and on the smaller number in permanent fostering. It takes a balanced approach to the day-to-day dilemmas associated with face-to-face contact as well as providing a host of other insights into what helps contact succeed.

RUSSELL HOUSE PUBLISHING 2002   154PP   ISBN 1 903855 09 8   £14.95 + £3.50 P&P

Adoption with Contact
Implications for policy and practice
Joan Fratter

Fratter's study is possibly the first of its kind to focus exclusively on the experience of adoption with contact in the cases of 32 children with special needs. The findings support the move towards greater openness, although the importance of using a child-centred approach in each situation is stressed.

BAAF 1996   281PP   ISBN 1 873868 37 5   £9.95 + £2.00 P&P

See You Soon
Contact with children looked after by local authorities
Edited by Hedi Argent

This anthology explores the "live" issues in planning and managing appropriate contact from a variety of viewpoints, illustrating them with case studies whenever possible. Contributions include an exploration of the history of contact arrangements; the legal framework; contact in the local authority setting; contact with children who have been abused; and planning for permanence with contact. Comprehensive and rich in information, this collection offers guidance, useful insights and recommendations for improving practice.

BAAF 1995   210PP   ISBN 1 873868 30 8   £10.95 + £3.50 P&P

Contact
Managing visits to children
Peg McCartt Hess and Kathleen Ohman Proch

Visiting is a key component of contact arrangements. This excellent handbook contains valuable guidance on good practice and equips proessionals with the strategies for arranging and supporting visiting plans.

BAAF 1993   88PP   ISBN 1 873868 12 X   £3.00 + £1.00 P&P

Order any of the above from **BAAF Publications, British Association for Adoption and Fostering, Skyline House, 200 Union Street, London SE1 0LX. Fax: 020 7593 2001**